THE ROOKIE
HANDBOOK

THE ROOKIE HANDBOOK

HOW TO BECOME THE OFFICER EVERY DEPARTMENT WANTS AND EVERY COMMUNITY NEEDS

E.J. COOPER

VALOR INK PUBLISHING

Cover Design by Front of The Class LLC

ISBN 979-8-218-29262-1

Printed in the United States of America.

"To the brave men and women who gave everything for the safety of others.

May your valor inspire and guide those who follow in

your footsteps."

Contents

Preface i

PART I: THE CALL TO SERVE

The Power of the Badge 3

Why Law Enforcement? 7

Reality of the Badge 9

Commitment to Serve 13

Rewards of Service 17

Call to Action 19

PART II: PREPARING FOR THE JOURNEY

Pathways to the Badge 25

Preparation 31

The Extra Mile 35

PART III: THE HIRING PROCESS

Getting Started 43

Screening & Evaluation 45

Final Steps 53

PART IV: FROM THE CLASSROOM TO THE STREETS

Into the Fray 57

The Academy 61

Field Training... 65

The First Year 71

PART V: THE BIGGER PICTURE

Scars of Duty... 77

Wellness 79

Leaving a Legacy... 85

Acknowledgments... 91

About the Author.. 93

Preface

Pursuing a career in law enforcement is an extensive process that will expose your vulnerabilities, test you mentally, and demand your utmost commitment. That's only the beginning. The real test comes after you've successfully completed the process and are out on your own, facing the complexities of the streets with a badge and a duty to serve.

I speak from experience. As a black man who has served as a law enforcement officer across multiple states, from bustling metropolitans to quiet suburbs, I've gone through these transitions firsthand. I've shouldered the responsibilities of a Patrol Officer, Field Training Officer (FTO), Defensive Tactics Instructor, Patrol Sergeant, and SWAT team member.

Over the years, I've helped guide aspiring officers and deputies through the gauntlet of a hiring process. This process can quickly become overwhelming unless you have a knowledgeable source to show you the way. Sure, one can turn to the internet for guidance, but it's not uncommon for this path to lead down a road of conflicting advice. At this point, confusion, doubt, and insecurity find fertile ground to take root.

I wrote this book to offer a step-by-step guide that demystifies the process of becoming a law enforcement officer. Beyond tips and tricks, it is a complete resource leading you through the hiring process, academy, and field training. Additionally, it lays a path to success once you are out on your own. Whether you're contemplating a calling in law enforcement or already on the path, this book will offer invaluable insight and support to help you become the officer every department wants, and every community needs.

In the following pages, I share experiences and insights from my career in law enforcement. I have altered names and geographical locations to respect privacy and maintain confidentiality. This ensures that the stories hold true to the spirit and lessons of my experiences while protecting the identities of those involved.

PART I:

THE CALL TO SERVE

The Power of the Badge

The power of the badge is profound, capable of altering destinies with a single encounter. I first truly understood this under the glare of red and blue lights on a summer evening during my high school years. A casual drive with friends to a house party became a stark introduction to a side of policing I had only heard of but never experienced firsthand.

As we approached the party, it was immediately apparent that our night was taking an unexpected turn.

"Damn, looks like the function got rolled," Dee said as we drove onto the street and saw police officers directing people out of the house.

"No point in trying to get through all this. Let's just swing around and check out that other spot," Mario said as he made a U-turn.

Suddenly, a swarm of patrol cars sped up to us and activated their lights. "Driver…put the car in park! Turn it off! Everyone inside, stick your hands out the window!" a cop ordered.

"Yo, are they pointing guns at us right now?" Dee nervously asked.

"I don't know, bro. Just keep looking forward and do whatever they say," I uttered, my words tense.

One by one, we were removed from the car, frisked, and seated along the curb. At the end of the ordeal, no contraband was found, and we were released without an explanation. What resulted in an insignificant waste of time for those officers was a life-changing event for us. At that moment, we were reduced to nothing more than suspects, our youthful excitement for the night ahead replaced by a deep sense of vulnerability.

Reflection and Resolve

This encounter could have been a catalyst for resentment, a push toward a path of defiance. Indeed, such interactions have swayed many, painting their perception of law enforcement with a single, broad stroke of distrust. However, my story took a different trajectory.

Rooted in my life were two figures who embodied the best of what law enforcement ought to be—family members who wore the uniform and served their community with honor and integrity. They were the counterbalance to the scales this encounter had so heavily tipped. They demonstrated that policing could be done with compassion and fairness and that the badge could symbolize both authority and service.

Reflecting on that night, I realized that the actions of those officers didn't have to define my perception of law enforcement. Instead, I could draw inspiration from the exemplary conduct of my relatives and strive to embody those same principles. This reflection turned a negative experience into a source of strength and determination.

Mission and Path

In the face of that night's trial, I found resolve rather than bitterness. It planted an aspiration to become a model of what an officer should be. I turned that chip on my shoulder into a cornerstone of a career built on fairness, courage, and genuine service. The best response to injustice, I realized, was to embody justice myself. That became my mission: to don the badge not as a shield for power but as a pledge to protect and to be the change I believed was necessary.

My path became clear. I would enter law enforcement to make a difference and to show that integrity and empathy could coexist with the authority of the badge. This mission drove me through the academy, onto the streets, and into the communities I served. Each day on the job was an opportunity to build trust, foster relationships, and correct the misconceptions that stem from negative encounters like the one I experienced.

I sought to mentor new recruits, sharing my story and encouraging them to understand the profound impact their actions could have on the lives of those they served. Through leading by example, I aimed to cultivate a culture of respect and empathy within the force, ensuring that every interaction upheld the honor and responsibility that comes with the badge.

Why Law Enforcement?

The heartbeat of law enforcement isn't found in the echo of sirens or the flash of lights—it's in the *why*. The reason you show up to work, the purpose behind the polished boots, the driving force that propels you forward when the burden of the uniform weighs heavy on your shoulders.

To those donning the uniform for the first time, I can't stress enough how important it is to know your *why*. It must be clear, compelling, and at the forefront of your consciousness. It is your anchor and the steadfast light amidst the fog of challenges that will inevitably arise. Your *why* isn't just a personal mantra; it's your promise to everyone you serve.

Understanding Your Why

Knowing your *why* means understanding the deep-seated motivations that drew you to this profession. Is it a commitment to justice, a desire to protect the vulnerable, or perhaps the aspiration to be a positive force in your community? Reflect on the experiences and values that led you to law enforcement. This clarity will sustain you through the trials and tribulations of the job, grounding you in moments of doubt and adversity.

The Promise of Service

Your *why* embodies the promise you make to your community every time you put on the uniform. It signifies your commitment to act with integrity, fairness, and compassion. This promise is to uphold the law and serve with honor. It is a pledge to be a steady presence in times of chaos, a source of comfort in moments of fear, and a symbol of justice in a world often marred by inequity.

Reaffirming Your Why

Throughout your career, regularly revisiting and reaffirming your *why* is crucial. Law enforcement demands can sometimes blur your initial motivations, leading to burnout or disillusionment. Take time to reflect on your journey, celebrate your achievements, and learn from your challenges. Reconnect with the core values that inspired you to pursue this path. This ongoing reflection ensures your *why* remains a vibrant and guiding force in your career.

Sharing Your Why

Sharing your *why* with colleagues and new recruits can be incredibly powerful. It reinforces your commitment and inspires others to reflect on their own motivations. In a profession where camaraderie and mutual support are vital, understanding and respecting each other's *whys* can strengthen team cohesion and morale. It fosters an environment where everyone is driven by a shared sense of purpose and dedication.

Living Your Why

Living your *why* means embodying your values in every action and decision. It means approaching each situation with the same passion and integrity that first led you to this profession. Whether you're interacting with a community member, mentoring a new recruit, or making a split-second decision in the field, let your *why* guide you. This alignment between your purpose and your actions will not only make you a more effective officer but also a respected and trusted figure in your community.

Reality of the Badge

The badge is more than an accessory to the uniform; it's a promise to the community. The weight of this promise is felt not in its ounces but in the gravity of the realities it encompasses. Officers regularly encounter humanity on its most harrowing days, often amidst cascades of tragedy and turmoil. It's a path where the fragility of life becomes a workplace reality, not just an abstract concept.

When I first envisioned a career in law enforcement, my mind painted scenes of high-octane chases and the clear-cut triumph of good over evil. Sure, I've had my fair share of these moments, but I learned that the reality was painted in more complex shades. It's not just about the adrenaline-fueled hot pursuits; it's about the nuanced art of human connection and the impact we officers have on those we come in contact with.

Beyond the Glamour

The not-so-glamorous aspects of the badge come to light in the silence that follows the sirens. The stark aftermath of a high-speed pursuit or the somber removal of crime scene tape reveals the weight of what officers bear witness to—scenes of violence, loss, and death that become etched in memory. Law enforcement professionals are often the first to step into situations where lives have been irrevocably altered, standing as the stoic constants amidst chaos and despair.

Then there's the everyday interactions that don't make headlines. The resolution of a neighborly dispute, helping a lost child find their way home, or comforting someone in distress.

These quieter moments, though less glamorous, are equally important and define the essence of service.

Public Perception

The badge also bears the weight of public perception—a duality of respect and skepticism. As an officer, you step into a narrative shaped by countless factors: media portrayals, community relationships, historical tensions, and individual experiences with law enforcement. Some will see you as a figure of safety, others as a symbol of fear. Navigating these perceptions requires an officer to be as adept in communication as they are in tactical skills.

Building trust within the community is an ongoing practice. It involves transparency, accountability, and consistent positive interactions. It's about showing the public that behind the badge is a person dedicated to serving and protecting, someone who listens and cares about their concerns. Public perception can be influenced by small acts of kindness and professionalism just as much as by significant, heroic deeds.

Drawing on my own experiences, I've worked in neighborhoods where officers have been slain in the line of duty, and officer-involved shootings have resulted in the deaths of suspects. I've witnessed firsthand the profound impact these incidents can have on a community. The friction generated in these environments is tangible. If left unaddressed, it can fester and deepen the divide between the community and law enforcement. We must understand and address this tension, transforming it into a catalyst for unity and positive change.

Off-Duty Struggles

The cumulative toll of experiences on the job shapes an officer, and usually spills over into the personal realm. Law enforcement officers grapple with one of the highest divorce rates among professions. The strain that the job places on relationships is considerable, often due to the irregular hours, the missed milestones, and the burden of experiences that can be difficult to communicate or leave at the door.

Moreover, the profession grapples with an alarming suicide rate. The veneer of stoicism that officers wear like armor can sometimes isolate them from seeking help or acknowledging their struggles. Mental health remains one of the most significant and critical challenges within the force. The psychological ramifications of constant exposure to trauma, the internalization of grief, and the high-stakes stress can erode even the most steadfast resolve.

Managing the personal impact involves balancing your duty and your personal life. It's essential to have a support system— whether it's family, friends, or fellow officers—to help you cope with the emotional toll of the job. Regular mental health check-ins can be crucial, whether through professional counseling or informal conversations with trusted peers.

Acknowledging the challenges of law enforcement is not a sign of weakness but a stride toward strength. It is an acceptance that the badge we wear is not an impervious shield but a human commitment. It comes with the understanding that we are not infallible guardians but human beings tasked with an extraordinary responsibility that we must face with care for our communities and ourselves.

Commitment to Serve

At the core of law enforcement lies a commitment that extends beyond the individual—it's a pledge to uphold the safety, rights, and dignity of the communities we serve. This commitment is the silent oath that echoes in the heart of every officer who has chosen this path for the right reasons.

A Multifaceted Role

To serve is a commitment to step into a role that is larger than oneself. This commitment requires a multifaceted approach. On the surface, it's about law enforcement, order maintenance, and response to emergencies. But dive deeper; you'll find it's equally about engagement, education, and empathy. We are as much guardians of peace as we are facilitators of community well-being.

This dual role can be challenging to maneuver. Officers must be ready to switch from enforcing the law to offering a hand of support, sometimes within the same call. It's about knowing when to stand firm, when to listen, when to lead, and when to be part of the team. The delicate balance between authority and assistance is one that we must constantly refine.

This balancing act requires continuous learning and adaptability. Every situation is unique, and the ability to read circumstances accurately and respond appropriately is a skill that must be honed. It's about having the wisdom to apply the right approach, whether de-escalating a conflict or reassuring a distressed community member.

Equity and Fairness

Moreover, the commitment to serve is about recognizing that each individual's experiences with law enforcement are shaped by their background, culture, and past encounters. It's crucial to be aware of our own inherent biases and continually strive to ensure that these preconceptions do not color our judgment.

We are all guilty of assuming things. However, we can provide equitable service to our communities by challenging those assumptions and self-reflecting. Cultural competence and implicit bias can help officers understand and navigate the diverse communities they serve more effectively. This concept can often become corroded throughout an officer's career, especially for those who work in harsher environments. But by keeping it at the forefront of memory, officers can build stronger, more trusting relationships with the public.

Long-Term Impact

The service we provide goes beyond the immediate. Every interaction has the potential to leave a lasting impression. We wield the power to instill trust or break it, to inspire or dishearten with every word and deed.

Reflecting on my life, I realize that my commitment to service has been my guiding principle. It has been the measure against which I assess my actions and decisions. It has been both my challenge and my reward. Ultimately, this commitment is not just about fulfilling duties—it's about honoring a sacred trust.

Understanding the long-term impact of our actions helps us remain mindful of the broader implications of our work. The relationships we build and the trust we foster can enhance community cooperation and support, which are essential for effective law enforcement. By consistently demonstrating integrity and compassion, we contribute to a positive legacy that endures beyond our individual careers.

Rewards of Service

The fabric of a law enforcement career is woven with threads of profound challenge, but amid those are interlaced strands of deep, enduring reward. These rewards often emerge in moments of crisis, where an officer's intervention is the difference between life and despair. They can also bloom in the quieter interactions like the gentle gratitude of those you've aided, the respectful nods from the elders in the community, and the wide-eyed admiration of children who see in you the heroes they dream of being.

Personal Fulfillment

For me, as a black man in uniform, there is a unique privilege in standing as a figure of possibility for kids who may not see many role models who look like them. It is a chance to redefine narratives and portray a figure worth aspiring to be like. This personal fulfillment goes beyond the immediate duties of the job—it is about being a beacon of hope and a living testament to what is possible.

The lighter moments of engaging in outreach and offering guidance may not carry the dramatic weight of life-or-death scenarios, but their impact is no less significant. These moments are opportunities to promote trust, inspire the next generation, and fortify the bridge between law enforcement and the public we serve. They remind us that every interaction has the potential to shape perceptions and build lasting relationships.

Whether participating in community events, mentoring the young, or simply being a positive presence in the neighborhood, these interactions contribute to community cohesion and mutual respect. They are the quiet, steady work that underpins the more visible aspects of policing.

Creating Change

The rewards of service in law enforcement are multifaceted. They resonate not just in the moment of action but echo into the lives we touch. They reverberate in the stories of those we've helped, the safer streets, and the peace of mind we provide to the community. They are present in the quiet pride that comes with knowing we've done our job well, with integrity and honor.

To wear the badge is to accept a life of service, and in that service, to discover profound and enduring rewards. It is to engage in a profession that, at its best, is about creating positive change— one interaction, one rescue, one child's smile at a time. The true measure of these rewards is found in the heartbeats that continue because of our intervention, in the breaths drawn in safety rather than fear, and in the community bonds strengthened by our commitment to serve.

Every act of service, no matter how small, contributes to the larger goal of community safety and trust. We build a foundation of respect and cooperation when we respond to calls, provide assistance, and engage with residents. These efforts create an environment where people feel safe and supported, developing a stronger, more resilient community.

As law enforcement officers, we can make a tangible difference in the lives of individuals and the broader community. This impact is the essence of the rewards of service—it is the legacy we build through our daily actions and interactions. It is the fulfillment of our duty and the realization of the profound influence we can have on the world around us.

Call to Action

In the silent reflection that follows the peak of sirens and the day's toil, one truth remains clear: a career in law enforcement is an unwavering declaration of courage and commitment. It is a profession defined by the nobility of its purpose and the profound impact it can have on society.

This noble path is etched with the promise of service, a promise that calls us to stand on the front lines of humanity's most challenging moments. It's a path that demands sacrifice, resilience, and an unyielding dedication to the principles of justice and protection. Yet, the rewards of this calling are immeasurable. They lie in lives saved, communities strengthened, and silent nods of respect from those we serve. They are found in the legacy we build and the peace we bring to troubled hearts.

Law enforcement is a career that allows us to be the signal of hope, the shield against chaos, and the bearer of compassion. It offers the chance to be a pivotal force in people's lives, often at times when they need it most. To serve within this profession is to be granted the honor of making a tangible difference every day, an opportunity few careers can genuinely claim.

Embracing the Journey

If within you burns the desire to contribute to something greater than yourself, protect, serve, and uphold the ideals that form the bedrock of a safe society, then the badge awaits. Answering this call means stepping into a tradition of valor, an enduring legacy of those who have donned the uniform before you. It means choosing to be part of a lineage woven into the fabric of our nation's history, which requires the best of us.

Stepping into this line of work is more than just accepting a job; it is committing to a way of life that demands courage, integrity, and unwavering dedication. This path is not for everyone. It is for those willing to face uncertainty and danger with resolve to be a source of strength and stability in times of chaos.

To fully embrace this profession, one must understand the weight of the responsibility that comes with the badge. It involves constant self-improvement. The journey requires a commitment to physical fitness, mental resilience, and continuous professional development. It means staying informed about new laws, techniques and community needs and adapting to the ever-evolving landscape of law enforcement.

This job will test you, but it will also reward you in profound and enduring ways. The satisfaction of knowing that you have made a difference and helped someone in their moment of need is unparalleled. The true rewards of this path are the respect earned from your peers and the community, the sense of pride in wearing the uniform, and the knowledge that you are part of something much larger than yourself.

Joining the Legacy

For those ready to accept this responsibility, know that the path is demanding, but the road is paved with a profound purpose. You are the future of law enforcement, the architects of community trust, and the guardians of the peace we cherish. Welcome the training, the challenges, and the opportunities that come with this role, and carry the torch of service with pride.

Let this book be your guide, your map through the complexities and rewards that the field of law enforcement holds. As you turn each page and step further into the reality of the badge, hold steadfast to your why, for it is the beacon that will guide you through the storms and into the calm of fulfilled duty.

PART II:

PREPARING FOR THE JOURNEY

Pathways to the Badge

The hiring process can be pursued through multiple routes, each offering advantages and challenges. By understanding the benefits and intricacies of each route, you can make an informed decision that aligns with your personal goals and professional aspirations.

Education

A common misconception is that a degree in criminal justice is a prerequisite for success in the field. However, this is far from the case.

1. **Diverse Educational Backgrounds:** I entered the academy without a formal education in criminal justice, a path not uncommon in the law enforcement community. Surprisingly, this did not place me at a disadvantage. During academy training and subsequent evaluations, I performed on par with, if not outperforming, colleagues who had invested years in criminal justice studies. The practical application of law enforcement duties relies less on theoretical knowledge and more on adaptability, critical thinking, and interpersonal skills—qualities that can be honed in myriad ways outside the classroom.

2. **Value of a Criminal Justice Degree:** This does not diminish the value of a criminal justice degree. A degree can be invaluable for those aiming for specific roles within the field, such as federal law enforcement positions or departments with explicit educational requirements. It provides a

solid foundation of knowledge and can enhance one's understanding of the legal system, ethics, and the societal context of policing.

3. **Variety of Degrees and Skills:** Law enforcement agencies value diversity in skills and backgrounds. Degrees in psychology, sociology, public administration, or even unrelated fields can bring unique perspectives and capabilities to the force. Life experiences, vocational training, and military service are also highly regarded, often equipping candidates with the resilience, leadership, and problem-solving skills essential for the demands of law enforcement.

Military

Another valuable pathway to consider is joining the military before entering law enforcement. This route offers unique benefits that can significantly enhance your readiness and qualifications for a career in law enforcement. I chose this pathway through the Marine Corps, and it has provided me with a solid foundation for my law enforcement career.

1. **Discipline and Structure:** The military instills a strong sense of discipline, structure, and responsibility. These qualities are directly transferable to a career in law enforcement, where adherence to rules, regulations, and a chain of command is crucial.

2. **Physical Fitness:** Military training emphasizes physical fitness, which is a critical component of law enforcement readiness. The rigorous physical training in the military ensures that you meet and often exceed the physical requirements needed for law enforcement.

3. **Leadership Skills:** The military provides extensive training and opportunities to lead in challenging situations.

These experiences develop your ability to make quick decisions, manage stress, and lead others effectively—skills invaluable in law enforcement.

4. **Experience Under Pressure:** Military service often involves operating in high-pressure environments, which prepares you for the stressful and sometimes dangerous situations encountered in law enforcement. This experience helps build mental resilience and remain calm under pressure.

5. **Veteran Preference:** Many law enforcement agencies give hiring preference to military veterans, recognizing the value of the skills and experiences gained during military service. This can provide an advantage in the competitive hiring process.

6. **Educational Benefits:** I utilized my GI Bill during the police academy and all throughout FTO. Having the added benefit of receiving BAH on top of my police salary was certainly a burden relief. Not all agencies offer this or even know about it, but many do. Do your due diligence by contacting the VA to maximize your benefits if this applies to you.

Corrections Deputy

Another viable pathway to a career in law enforcement is starting as a corrections deputy and working inside jails before transitioning to patrolling the streets. This route offers a unique set of experiences and skills that can be highly beneficial for a career in law enforcement.

1. **Communication Skills:** Effective communication is crucial in law enforcement. Corrections deputies regularly interact with inmates, mediating disputes and ensuring

compliance with facility rules. This helps develop clear, assertive, and empathetic communication skills.

2. **Understanding the Justice System:** Starting as a corrections deputy provides an in-depth understanding of the justice system from a different perspective, enhancing your knowledge and effectiveness as a law enforcement officer.

3. **Professional Relationships:** Starting in corrections allows for building professional relationships within the department and the broader law enforcement community. Networking with fellow officers and supervisors can open doors for career advancement.

Self-Sponsorship

Alternatively, some individuals choose to attend the academy independently. Whether it be because they prefer to take the initiative on their own terms or because they have not yet secured agency sponsorship. This path can also lead to a rewarding career in law enforcement, and it comes with its own set of advantages:

1. **Flexibility:** Attending the academy independently allows you to apply to multiple agencies during or after your training, allowing you to choose the agency that best fits your career goals and values.

2. **Preparation:** Completing the academy before applying to agencies can make you a more attractive candidate, as it demonstrates your commitment to the profession and reduces the training investment required by potential employers.

3. **Networking:** While in the academy, you can network with instructors, fellow cadets, and visiting officers from various agencies, opening doors to job opportunities.

Agency Sponsorship

The traditional and most common route into law enforcement is to get hired by an agency before attending the academy. With this path, the agency sponsors you to attend the academy, covering the costs and paying you a salary during your training. This route offers several benefits:

1. **Financial Support:** The agency covers your tuition and other academy-related expenses. In addition, you receive a salary while you train, which can alleviate financial stress.
2. **Job Security:** Being hired before the academy means you have a job waiting for you once you graduate. This provides a clear, stable career path from the outset.
3. **Agency Integration:** Starting your training with agency sponsorship allows you to build relationships with your future colleagues and understand the specific expectations and culture of the agency you serve.

Choosing the right pathway for your career is a pivotal decision. Each route—whether traditional education, military service, self-sponsored academy training, agency sponsorship, or starting as a corrections deputy—offers advantages and experiences that can uniquely prepare you for the job's demands. You can select the pathway that best suits you by carefully considering your circumstances, strengths, and career goals.

Remember, the ultimate goal is to equip yourself with the skills, knowledge, and resilience necessary to uphold the values of justice and service.

Preparation

Preparation is the cornerstone of success in any profession, and law enforcement is no exception. Entering the field requires more than just physical readiness; it demands a holistic approach that encompasses mental, emotional, and physical preparation. By dedicating time and effort to preparation, you set the foundation for a successful and fulfilling career.

Physical Preparation

Unfortunately, there is often a vast difference in physical preparedness among recruits in the academy. For some, the workouts in the academy are merely a warmup for their workout after the academy day ends. For others, the academy is the pinnacle of their fitness level. The structured workouts, high standards, and camaraderie during physical endeavors shape many into the best condition of their careers. However, once the structured environment of the academy is left behind, many officers neglect to maintain this level of fitness.

This decline in physical conditioning is not just a personal risk. It jeopardizes the safety of fellow squadmates on patrol and the community they serve. The physical demands of law enforcement—chasing a suspect, restraining an assailant, or responding to emergencies—require officers to be in peak physical condition. A lapse in fitness can mean the difference between life and death in critical situations.

The fitness requirements of the academy should only be looked at as a stepping stone, not the pinnacle of your fitness prowess. From there, you should seek out finding a home gym for jiu-jitsu and weightlifting (if your department does not have a gym), and I would even add finding a shooting range as part of this physical discussion. It is essential to have all of these physical attributes aligned.

Maintaining a high level of fitness is crucial for your health and safety, as well as the effectiveness and safety of your entire team. The responsibility of an officer extends beyond personal well-being to include the well-being of colleagues and the community. The commitment to physical preparation must be a lifestyle, not just a temporary goal. There are many forms of training you can pursue; however, the two I hold in the highest regard would be the following:

1. **Jiu Jitsu:** BJJ is an invaluable discipline for law enforcement officers. It teaches control, leverage, and submission techniques that can be crucial in apprehending suspects without excessive force...which is a hot topic nowadays. Regular training in jiu-jitsu not only enhances physical fitness but also improves mental discipline and situational awareness. Finding a local jiu jitsu school and committing to regular training can significantly enhance your ability to handle physical confrontations effectively and safely.

2. **Strength and Conditioning:** The gym goes without saying, but if you are not regularly training, now is the time. There are plenty of programs out there that specialize in training for law enforcement. These will help you perform the job's physical demands and, more importantly, help prevent injuries common in this line of work.

Mental Preparation

The mental and emotional challenges of law enforcement are as demanding, if not more, than the physical ones. Mental resilience is paramount. Developing the ability to cope with the demands and aftermath of this job in a positive way involves preparation beforehand. Although you might not recognize the signs of mental fatigue, anxiety, etc., in yourself and your colleagues early on in your career, it's great to get ahead of the curve.

1. **Mindfulness and Meditation:** Techniques such as mindfulness and meditation can be invaluable tools. These practices not only help in managing the stresses inherent to law enforcement but also in making critical decisions under pressure. Regular engagement in these practices can enhance your psychological readiness and emotional intelligence, which are crucial skills in the field and in managing home life off-duty.

2. **Regular Physical Exercise:** Physical activity helps reduce stress, improve mood, and increase overall well-being. Activities like running, weightlifting, yoga, or jiu-jitsu can be beneficial. Physical fitness is not only essential for job performance but also for maintaining mental health.

3. **Healthy Diet and Sleep:** Maintaining a balanced diet and ensuring adequate sleep are foundational to mental health. A well-nourished body and a well-rested mind are better equipped to handle stress and perform under pressure.

4. **Engaging in Hobbies and Interests:** Maintaining hobbies and interests outside work helps officers relax and unwind. Whether golfing, gardening, or playing a musical instrument, finding joy in activities unrelated to law enforcement is essential.

5. **Building a Support Network:** Developing a solid support network of family, friends, and colleagues provides emotional support and a sense of community. Having trusted individuals to talk to can make a significant difference in mental health.

Do Your Homework

It's essential to do extensive research. You should have a clear understanding of the department you're applying to and the broader context in which it operates—the state laws, the local government, and the community's views on law enforcement. This knowledge will prepare you for the hiring process and give you insight into the environment you'll potentially be working in.

Engaging in ride-alongs is an invaluable part of your research. These firsthand experiences offer a glimpse into the daily realities of policing, allowing you to ask critical questions about department morale, operational procedures, and the work-life balance within the force. Questions about vacation policies, overtime practices, and the morale among officers can provide a deeper understanding of the department's culture and values.

Lastly, it's wise not to limit your options to a single department. The competitive nature of law enforcement hiring processes means that not every candidate will be successful on their first attempt. Applying to multiple departments increases your chances of entry into the field. Remember, it's possible to transfer to your preferred department once you've gained experience and proven your capabilities as an officer.

The Extra Mile

To truly excel in this career, it's essential to welcome the roles of mentorship and community engagement. These elements enhance your professional development and strengthen the bond between law enforcement and the communities we serve. By going above and beyond, you can make a lasting impact beyond your immediate duties.

Mentorship

The relationships forged along this path are paramount. It is a path where the collective wisdom, support, and camaraderie of those who share our commitment can significantly impact our success and fulfillment in the profession. Networking within the law enforcement community and actively seeking mentorship are not merely advantageous; they are essential pillars that support career development and personal growth.

Engaging with the law enforcement community through networking is more than a professional formality—it is an investment in your career's future. These relationships offer diverse perspectives on policing, insights into various specializations, and firsthand accounts of navigating the field's challenges. By connecting with peers, supervisors, and experienced professionals at training sessions, conferences, and community events, you gain access to a wealth of knowledge and experiences that can guide your career decisions and prepare you for the demands of the job.

This network also provides a support system crucial for enduring the emotional and physical rigors of law enforcement work.

The unique bond shared among officers, rooted in shared experiences and challenges, offers a level of understanding and support difficult to find elsewhere. Within this community, many find the encouragement and resilience needed to thrive in their roles.

I can attest to the transformative power of mentorship in law enforcement. Throughout my life, I have been fortunate to have mentors whose guidance, wisdom, and support have been instrumental in reaching the point I am at today. These mentors have shared their insights and experiences and challenged me to grow, adapt, and strive for excellence in all aspects of my duties. Their influence has been a beacon, guiding me through the complexities and demands of the job, and I genuinely believe I would not be where I am now without their guidance.

The search for a mentor should be a thoughtful and intentional decision. Look for individuals who embody the qualities you aspire to, whose career paths inspire you, and whose ethical and professional standards align with your own. A mentor can be someone from your immediate environment or a connection made through your broader network. The essence of this relationship is trust, respect, and a mutual commitment to growth.

Mentorship and networking are not merely stepping stones at the beginning of your law enforcement career but continuous sources of development and enrichment. The field of law enforcement is ever-evolving, and staying connected ensures you remain informed about the latest developments, innovations, and best practices. These relationships facilitate lifelong learning and help you through your career's progression from initial training to potential leadership roles.

The significance of networking and mentorship in law enforcement cannot be overstated. They are the bedrock upon which a successful and rewarding career is built, providing guidance, support, and opportunities for growth. As you progress in your career, remember the value of these connections and consider how you, in turn, can mentor others. By doing so, you contribute to your personal development and the strength and vitality of the law enforcement community as a whole.

Community Engagement

The essence of law enforcement transcends the physical confines of patrolling and investigating; it is deeply rooted in the community's social and cultural fabric. Officers often find themselves not just as keepers of peace but as integral members of the community they serve. In areas, particularly those with a significant military presence, it's not uncommon to find officers with no prior ties to the area they patrol. While this isn't inherently problematic, a profound understanding of the community's dynamics, history, and culture can significantly enhance an officer's effectiveness and the quality of service provided.

For those aspiring to a career in law enforcement, engaging with the community even before wearing the badge can be incredibly beneficial. Volunteering and participating in local events offer prospective officers a unique insight into the community's heartbeat. These activities allow for a genuine connection with the public outside the traditional law enforcement context, breaking down barriers and fostering trust.

Such involvement can take many forms, from participating in neighborhood clean-up campaigns to volunteering at local shelters, joining community advisory boards, or engaging in youth mentorship programs. These experiences not only contribute positively to the community but also equip prospective officers with a nuanced understanding of the people they will serve. This proactive engagement demonstrates a commitment to public service that transcends the obligations of the badge.

To serve effectively, officers must grasp the underlying currents that shape community life. This means recognizing the diverse tapestry of cultures, values, and expectations that exist within a community. For those new to an area, especially in cities with diverse populations or significant military influence, this understanding is crucial. It involves learning about the community's historical context, the issues it faces, and the local figures and institutions that play pivotal roles in community life.

Building relationships from the outset is about listening and learning. It's about showing up with an open mind and a genuine willingness to understand. Engage in dialogues at community meetings, participate in local traditions and celebrations, and be present in places of communal gathering. These interactions offer invaluable insights into the community's needs and expectations and reveal how law enforcement can best support and protect its members.

Community engagement fosters a sense of belonging and mutual respect. It allows officers to become familiar faces rather than distant figures of authority, facilitating cooperation and collaboration. When officers invest time in understanding and contributing to their communities, they lay the foundation for a partnership based on trust and respect. This partnership is vital for effective policing, ensuring that officers are seen not just as law enforcers but as dedicated guardians of the community's well-being.

Engaging with the community before donning the badge is not just beneficial—it's essential. It lays the groundwork for a career built on effective communication, empathy, and mutual respect. As prospective law enforcement officers, your commitment to public service begins with your involvement in the community. By taking the time to understand the area you'll potentially be working in and building relationships from the outset, you set the stage for a fulfilling and impactful career dedicated to serving and protecting with knowledge, compassion, and integrity.

2020 was an interesting year for law enforcement...to say the least. The challenges were unprecedented, from navigating a global pandemic to responding to widespread social unrest. This photo captures a moment from that turbulent year when adaptability, resilience, and a steadfast commitment to duty were more important than ever.

PART III:

THE HIRING PROCESS

Getting Started

Entering this career requires dedication, resilience, and a deep-seated commitment to serve. Central to this path is the hiring process—a rigorous pathway that tests your physical readiness, mental acuity, emotional stability, and ethical integrity. Maneuvering through the intricacies of this process is imperative for aspiring officers, as it evaluates not only your ability to perform the duties of an officer but also your character, judgment, and potential to uphold the values of the department you wish to work for.

The Application

The first step is the application process, which might shock those who have never applied to a government position due to its extensiveness and intrusion. This initial interaction is your opportunity to make a strong impression on potential employers, setting the tone for your candidacy.

Law enforcement applications require an extensive collection of information, including family history, educational background, employment history, specific qualifications, and more. Departments are looking for candidates who demonstrate attention to detail, honesty, and the ability to follow instructions precisely.

Before filling out your application, gather all necessary documents and information. This will include phone numbers and addresses for all your references, identifying documents, educational certificates, military service records, and more. Even if the initial application does not require this information, it will be requested later during the backgrounds process.

The key to this portion of the process is to present yourself as a candidate who supersedes the basic requirements and stands out amongst the rest.

Written Examinations

The written exam is typically the first step after your application has been approved. It is designed to assess your cognitive ability with questions ranging from reading comprehension, problem-solving, critical thinking, spatial orientation, and more.

Now, before you go out and start prepping as if you are trying to get into law school, let me save you the trouble. This is not the SATs, ASVAB, etc. In short, these exams test your ability to receive, process, and articulate information correctly.

Although some departments administer their own exam, I've taken many, and they all tend to have commonalities. The most common exam I have encountered is the NCJOSI[2]. I recommend viewing this test if you want to get an idea of what law enforcement exams are like.

Fitness Test

Many agencies, but not all, administer some form of a fitness test early in the hiring process. It's important to emphasize that these tests represent the bare minimum standard. Preparing for it should not be the pinnacle of your physical achievement. This entry point is merely designed to verify that you can meet the job's demands.

As with all steps throughout this process, the fitness test reflects your preparedness and commitment. Suppose you have any doubts about your ability to meet these minimum standards. In this case, the responsibility falls on you to take proactive steps to improve your fitness level. Every hiring process witnesses candidates who falter at this stage, not due to a lack of potential but inadequate preparation...don't let this be you.

Screening & Evaluation

The screening and evaluation phase combines various assessments scrutinizing your background, psychological health, and integrity. From the thorough background investigation to the revealing polygraph exam, each step serves to verify your suitability for the demanding role you wish to fulfill. Preparing for these evaluations will help you complete this challenging phase confidently and clearly, bringing you one step closer to achieving your goal.

Background Investigation

The background investigation will take a deeper look into the details you've provided in your application and Personal History Questionnaire (PHQ). This includes examining your work history, family and friends, financial records, social media presence, and legal issues to assess your suitability for a law enforcement career.

In the pursuit of honesty and transparency throughout this step, there's an equally important principle to consider: wisdom. It's natural to feel overwhelmed when faced with detailed questions on the PHQ, a reaction that might prompt you to err on the side of caution to an extreme degree.

I can still recall when I filled out my first PHQ. Driven by a mixture of diligence and paranoia, I answered "yes" to several questions just to be on the safe side. A particular example involved a question about whether I had ever stolen items from an employer. Reflecting on a time in the Marines when I took cleaning supplies from work to my barracks room for a 'field day' inspection, I detailed this incident in my application. Despite returning the supplies, I was uncertain if this action might be interpreted as theft by the department to which I was applying. As I later learned through discussions with my background investigator, this was an unnecessary inclusion—a moment of overthinking born out of a desire to be overtly transparent.

This experience highlights a crucial lesson: while honesty is paramount, be smart about it. By no means am I telling you to lie— just be smart.

Here are some strategies to find this balance effectively:

1. **Understand the Question's Intent:** Before answering a question where you're unsure if an incident applies, consider the purpose behind the inquiry. Departments seek to identify behaviors that signify ethical or legal concerns, not minor or irrelevant transgressions.

2. **Seek Clarity When Needed:** If you find yourself overthinking a response, it may be helpful to seek clarification. While it's not always possible to ask the hiring department directly, you can consult with mentors or individuals who have successfully completed the process for their insight.

3. **Reflect Before You Respond:** Take the time to reflect on your experiences and how they've shaped your understanding of responsibility, integrity, and service. This reflection can guide you in determining which aspects of your history are most pertinent to share.

4. **Be Prepared to Discuss:** For any situation you disclose, be prepared to discuss it openly and thoughtfully with your background investigator. This moment allows you to demonstrate your honesty and explain how you've learned from your mistakes, grown mature, etc. Ownership is

crucial. The last thing you want to do here is make excuses or downplay an incident.

Most departments these days have applicants submit their PHQ electronically after giving them a week or two to complete it. This was not the case when I first got hired. We completed ours in a classroom full of other applicants. I remember taking a huge hit to my self-esteem when half the class blew through theirs and turned it in with a smile on their face. Let's just say I had a lot more than them to explain on my PHQ packet. I walked away from that classroom questioning if I was even worthy enough for this career...yet here I am.

Remember, the goal of this step is not to scrutinize every minor misstep in your past but to gauge your suitability for a career that demands a high degree of ethical conduct and responsibility. I know several great officers who did not make it through their initial hiring process due to things on their background. They waited a year, two, even longer in some instances, and their persistence and demonstration of growth earned them a career.

Interview

The interview is a pivotal component of the law enforcement hiring process, designed to evaluate your communication skills, judgment, ethical reasoning, and overall suitability for a career in policing. This face-to-face interaction allows the hiring panel to get a sense of who you are beyond the resume, probing into your motivations, your understanding of the role, and how you handle challenging situations.

Typically, the interview consists of a panel of command staff, patrol supervisors, and senior officers. The questions range from hypothetical scenarios requiring quick yet thoughtful decision-making to discussions on past experiences demonstrating your character and values. The panel is looking for evidence of critical thinking, moral integrity, a commitment to service, your knowledge of the department, and most of all what makes you stand out amongst the other applicants.

Strategies for Effective Communication:

1. **Preparation:** Familiarize yourself with common interview questions and practice your responses. Understanding the mission and values of the department you're applying to can help tailor your answers to reflect alignment with their goals. Also...make sure you KNOW WHO THE CHIEF OR SHERIFF IS! Sounds like an obvious one, but you'd be surprised.

2. **Be Concise and Clear:** Articulate your thoughts in a structured manner. Avoid rambling and ensure your answers directly address the question asked.

3. **Use Examples:** Whenever possible, draw on real-life experiences to support your answers. This provides evidence of your claims and helps the panel get to know you better.

4. **Stay Calm and Composed:** Interviews can be stressful, but maintaining composure is key. Take a moment to think before you answer. Don't be afraid to ask for clarification if you're unsure about a question.

5. **Show Your Personality:** While being professional is important, don't be afraid to let your genuine self shine through. Law enforcement agencies are looking for individuals who can connect with the community they serve.

6. **Ask Questions:** Prepare a few thoughtful questions at the end of the interview. This demonstrates your interest in the role and the department.

Sample Interview Questions:

1. Tell us about yourself. (Your response to this should be a synopsis of your life that highlights pivotal moments and significant traits that will set you apart from other applicants. Find a way to tie everything back to the position you're applying for).
2. Why do you want to pursue a career in law enforcement, and specifically with our department?
3. Can you describe a situation where you had to make a quick decision in a high-pressure environment? What was the outcome?
4. How would you handle a conflict with a fellow officer or a superior?
5. How do you define integrity, and how have you demonstrated it in your personal or professional life?
6. Given the current discussions about police reform, what are your views on community policing?

Preparing for the oral board interview is about more than rehearsing answers—it's about reflecting on your experiences, understanding your motivations, and being ready to engage in a meaningful dialogue about your future in law enforcement. Be prepared. Be honest. And be confident.

Psychological Exam

The psychological evaluation typically includes written tests and an interview with a psychologist. These evaluations ensure that candidates have the mental and emotional stability suitable for the job. If you are the type of person who hates taking tests...brace yourself. These tests typically have well over 300 questions. Then there's the added bonus of many of the questions being repeated, just worded differently.

Honesty is crucial, just as it is in other stages of the hiring process. Attempting to present an idealized version of yourself can be counterproductive because psychologists are trained to detect inconsistencies and discern whether candidates are being forthright. It's essential to be genuine and transparent during this assessment to ensure that you accurately portray yourself.

While it's natural to feel some anxiety about this assessment, try to approach it with calmness. Stress can impact your responses, so utilize stress-reduction techniques that work for you.

Polygraph Exam

The polygraph is used to verify the truthfulness of your application and statements throughout the hiring process. It measures physiological responses to questions that may indicate deception.

1. **Understand the Purpose:** Recognize that the polygraph is a tool to ensure candidates are being honest about their history and qualifications. It is not designed to trick you but to confirm the integrity of your application.
2. **Stay Calm:** Nervousness can affect the results of a polygraph. Practice relaxation techniques and remember that being truthful is the simplest way to pass the test.
3. **Clarify Misunderstandings:** If any questions during the polygraph are unclear, ask for clarification. Ensuring you fully understand each question will help you provide clear and truthful answers.

Once you've passed the psychological and polygraph exams, take a deep breath as you roll the corner into the home stretch. I'm not saying that you can drop your pack and get complacent, but the last step in the process is the medical exam, and all you really have to do for this step is not miss your appointment. I have never known anyone to fail this part of the process (I apologize if you're reading this and you've failed it…). From my understanding, you can only fail if you piss hot or have some serious underlying health condition that gets discovered.

Final Steps

Medical Exam

The medical examination is typically the last step in the hiring process. This examination is a standard procedure to ensure you meet the physical health requirements necessary for duty. It will likely include a general physical check-up, vision and hearing tests, and a drug screening. The step confirms that you have no medical conditions that would preclude you from performing as a law enforcement officer. It's a straightforward process that serves as the final confirmation of your physical readiness for your future career.

Official Job Offer

You likely received a conditional job offer somewhere along the process. This offer was dependent upon the successful completion of the remaining evaluations. With all conditions met, the official offer is the department's affirmation of your suitability and readiness to join the force.

You now stand at the threshold of a definitive transition in your life: the transition from candidate to prospective law enforcement officer. As you accept the offer, you accept the charge to serve with courage, to continue evolving, and to carry the badge with honor. Remember, this is not the conclusion of your path but the commencement of a profound and impactful profession.

PART IV:

FROM THE CLASSROOM TO THE STREETS

Into the Fray

The radio crackled to life, and the dispatcher's voice was as crisp as it was clinical: "All units be advised of a homicide that just occurred out of Metro Division. Suspect armed with a handgun, last seen fleeing eastbound on Magnolia Avenue." My heart pounded a relentless rhythm, not out of fear, but from the rush of adrenaline surging throughout my body as the realization of my current circumstance set in…this was no classroom scenario. It was my first week of Field Training—real calls, real consequences.

I glanced at my FTO (Field Training Officer), his seasoned eyes already scanning the horizon. Just hours earlier, my biggest worry had been memorizing my call sign, not intercepting a murderer. I tried to remember the tactics drilled into us at the academy. Still, the lessons felt distant and abstract in the face of raw urgency.

The streets had been eerily quiet until now, a deceptive calm where I had been failing to spot even the most basic traffic infractions that my FTO pointed out with frustrating ease. "Focus," he had said, "Anticipate." Yet here I was, lost—not just in location but in the sudden shift from theory to an alarming reality.

An update from dispatch interrupted my OODA loop as I tried to process my next move. "Suspect is believed to be heading to his ex-girlfriend's residence on 1200 Elm Street." 1200 Elm Street—where the sun was now painting the buildings with the first light of trouble.

"Isn't that address right over there?" I pointed, my voice much steadier than I felt. "Fuck yeah," my FTO confirmed with a smirk that hinted at the excitement he harbored for moments like this. Whether it was fait or mere coincidence, I had navigated us to the exact target location for the suspect.

Without question, I hastily followed my FTO's instruction to pull over. Our new position had the perfect balance of cover and visual of the target address. I then watched as he donned his tactical vest and helmet with methodical precision, a contrast to my fumbling hands as I prepared a beanbag shotgun for a less-lethal option. The ordinary weight of my vest suddenly felt like a mantle of responsibility I was only beginning to understand.

A tense moment as my FTO and I set up a perimeter, locking down the scene in pursuit of a homicide suspect. The gravity of the situation is profound as we prepare for the unknown. My FTO's experience guides our every move while I quickly adapt to the reality of policing. This early experience in my career stressed the seriousness of the role.

The Academy

Before hitting the streets and facing incidents like the one just shared, you must graduate from the police academy. The police academy is where the transition from civilian to officer truly begins. It's an environment designed to test your limits, build your skills, and prepare you for the complex and demanding world of law enforcement. From day one, you'll realize that the academy is not just about learning the law; it's about transforming into a disciplined, competent, and ethical officer ready to serve the community.

The curriculum covers a wide range of topics, including criminal law, traffic enforcement, investigation techniques, and community policing. You'll spend countless hours in classrooms, absorbing knowledge that forms the backbone of your future responsibilities.

The learning doesn't stop in the classroom either. Along with learning the law, you'll spend extensive time training skills from firearms, driving (EVOC), and arrest and control (defensive tactics).

Alongside the academic work, you'll face physical training designed to push your endurance, strength, and agility to new heights. This physical aspect prepares you for law enforcement's demanding and often unpredictable nature.

Lastly, practical scenarios play a crucial role in your training. These simulations—from traffic stops to domestic disputes—are designed to put your classroom knowledge to the test. They help you develop critical thinking skills, quick decision-making, and staying calm under pressure. You'll also learn the importance of discipline and routine, with uniform and weapon inspections, drill sessions, and a regimented schedule becoming daily fixtures. This discipline is not just about following orders; it's about internalizing the values of respect, responsibility, and reliability.

Volunteering for scenarios is particularly important. Some classmates may shy away from volunteering, allowing others to get extra reps in their place. This reluctance can be detrimental. The only way to improve and build confidence in your skills is through repetition. Avoiding scenarios may feel safer in the short term, but it ultimately sets you back in the long run. Embrace these opportunities to practice, make mistakes, and learn from them in a controlled environment. Each scenario you participate in is a chance to refine your techniques, learn from feedback, and prepare for real-life situations.

Here are some of the key challenges in the academy and strategies for success:

1. **Physical Training:** Although academies vary, most regularly engage in intense exercise. As discussed in the Preparation chapter, being physically prepared will make the transition smoother and reduce the risk of injury.

2. **Academic Workload:** The academic workload is substantial, and the pressure to perform can be overwhelming. Develop a study schedule, take good notes, and don't hesitate to ask for help from instructors or peers if you're struggling with the material.

3. **Teamwork and Peer Dynamics:** You'll be in close quarters with your classmates, and teamwork is essential. However, this environment can also lead to conflicts. Learning to work effectively with a diverse group of people,

managing conflicts professionally, and supporting each other is vital.

4. **Discipline:** Follow instructions carefully, meticulously maintain your uniform and equipment, and adhere to the schedule. Build these habits now so that it becomes second nature throughout your career.

5. **Adaptability and Resilience:** Adapt to new information and changing circumstances. Law enforcement is dynamic, and your ability to remain flexible and responsive will be tested. Along with this comes the resilience to cope with setbacks and failures. Not every day will be easy, and not every test will be passed on the first try. Learn from your mistakes, stay focused on your goals, and keep pushing forward.

6. **Skills:** Some people will breeze through skills training in the academy, while others will struggle. This is just the nature of the beast, and there's no way around it. Latch on to those who excel in areas you struggle in, whether lining up next to the best shooter on the range or partnering up with the most proficient in arrest and control.

As you encounter the challenges and demands of the police academy, always keep your 'why' at the forefront. Remember the commitment you made to serve and protect your community. Your 'why' is the driving force that will sustain you through the toughest days and the most strenuous drills. It's the reason you chose this path and the motivation that will keep you moving forward.

Equally important is focusing on what you can control. Show up on time, maintain a positive attitude, and give your best effort in everything you do. These elements require effort, not skill. They are within your control and demonstrate your dedication and professionalism. By consistently showing up prepared, working hard, and maintaining a positive demeanor, you set a strong foundation for your success.

Field Training

Field Training is a critical phase to becoming a fully-fledged law enforcement officer. It bridges the gap between the controlled environment of the academy and the unpredictable nature of real-world policing. This is where your classroom knowledge and physical training are tested, theory meets practice, and you begin developing the competence and confidence necessary for effective law enforcement.

During Field Training, you'll be paired with a Field Training Officer (FTO) who will mentor and evaluate you. This period is not only about learning the ropes but also about understanding the profound responsibility that comes with wearing the badge. It's a time to absorb as much as possible from experienced officers, to learn from every call and incident, and to refine the skills that will define your career.

The Structure of Field Training

Field Training is meticulously structured to ensure new officers transition smoothly from the academy to full duty. Field Training programs vary by department but generally last between 12 to 16 weeks. This period is often divided into phases, each designed to build upon the previous, gradually increasing the responsibility and expectations of the tasks you undertake.

Here's a typical breakdown:

1. **Phase One:** Introduction and Observation

- Duration: 1-2 weeks
- Focus: Familiarization with the department's procedures, policies, and the geographical area of your patrol.
- Activities: Shadowing your FTO, observing calls and responses, and understanding the department's daily operations.

2. **Phase Two:** Active Participation
   - Duration: 4-6 weeks
   - Focus: Gradually taking on more responsibilities under the close supervision of your FTO.
   - Activities: Handling calls, making traffic stops, and conducting preliminary investigations with guidance.

3. **Phase Three:** Increased Responsibility
   - Duration: 4-6 weeks
   - Focus: Taking the lead on calls and incidents while your FTO provides oversight and support.
   - Activities: Managing more complex situations and demonstrating decision-making abilities.

4. **Phase Four:** Final Evaluation
   - Duration: 2-4 weeks
   - Focus: Evaluating your readiness to operate independently.
   - Activities: Performing all duties with minimal intervention from your FTO and receiving final assessments and feedback.

Field Training Officer

At the heart of Field Training is the FTO. Your FTO is a seasoned officer responsible for guiding, mentoring, and evaluating you throughout this stage. The relationship between you and your FTO is pivotal; they are there to provide support, offer feedback, and help you integrate into the department's culture and procedures. An FTO serves as a role model, demonstrating the standards of conduct, decision-making, and professionalism expected in the field.

However, it's important to understand the reality of FTOs. While many are exceptional mentors and role models, others may fall short. FTOs are human, and their personalities, teaching styles, and attitudes vary widely. Some FTOs may be incredibly supportive and insightful, helping you grow and develop with constructive feedback and encouragement. Conversely, some may be unsuited for the role, engaging in demeaning behavior or simply lacking the skills to effectively mentor. It's crucial to use your sound judgment during this time and remember that your experience with an FTO is temporary.

Keep your head up, stay focused on your goals, and understand that even negative experiences can provide valuable lessons. Most of all, "drink the Kool-Aid," as they say. Even if you don't mesh well with your FTO, drink the Kool-Aid (play the part) to ensure you get off training as quickly as possible.

Common Challenges

The challenges of Field Training are numerous, but so are the growth opportunities. You'll face real-life situations that require quick thinking, adaptability, and resilience. You'll experience the highs of positively impacting your community and the lows of confronting the harsh realities of the job. Through it all, your focus should remain on building a solid work ethic, professionalism, and integrity foundation.

Here are some common challenges trainees face in Field Training:

1. **Adapting to Real-World Situations:** Transitioning from controlled scenarios to unpredictable real-world situations requires quick thinking and adaptability.
2. **Handling Criticism and Feedback:** Constant criticisms of your every move from your FTO can be challenging. Develop a thick skin, take feedback constructively, and use it as a tool for growth.
3. **Maintaining Confidence:** It's common to feel over-whelmed and question your abilities. Remember, making mistakes is part of the learning process; focus on learning and moving forward.
4. **Mental Fatigue:** Long hours, shift changes, and high-stress situations will lead to fatigue. Manage your stress by keeping your home life intact as best as possible and main-taining a healthy lifestyle to fuel you through this challenging stage.

As in the academy, focusing on what you can control—showing up on time, maintaining a positive attitude, and putting in your best effort—will significantly influence your success. These actions require effort, not skill, and demonstrate your dedication and professionalism.

Remember, the challenges and scrutiny of Field Training are temporary. The lessons you learn and the experiences you gain during this period will be invaluable as you advance in your career. Absorb as much knowledge as possible from your FTO and peers and remain resilient when facing difficulties.

As you go through the ups and downs of Field Training, keep your end goal in sight. Life on the other side—being a solo cop, making independent decisions, and serving your community—is worth weathering the storm. The skills, confidence, and resilience you develop during Field Training will lay a strong foundation for a successful and fulfilling career in law enforcement. Stay focused, stay committed, and remember that this is just another step along your way to becoming the officer you aspire to be.

The First Year

The first year as a law enforcement officer is a transformative period setting the tone for your career. It's a time when you transition from the structured training environment to the responsibilities and challenges of independent duty. The experiences and habits you develop during this year will significantly influence your professional growth and reputation.

Navigating the first year successfully requires maintaining the discipline and habits you developed during training, setting personal and professional goals, and continuously striving for improvement. It's also about building on your foundation, managing stress, establishing a positive reputation, and forming meaningful relationships within the department and the community.

Building on Your Foundation

Maintaining the discipline and routines you've done thus far is essential. Continue to show up on time, maintain your uniform and equipment, and follow procedures diligently. Consistency in these areas demonstrates your reliability and dedication to the job.

Some key ways to set yourself up for success are:

1. **Set Goals:** Establish clear, achievable goals for your first year. Focus on mastering specific skills, building relationships within your department, and contributing to community policing.

2. **Stay Hungry:** Approach each day with a growth mindset and curiosity. Be open to new experiences and willing to learn from everyone around you.

3. **Work-Life Balance:** Establish a healthy work-life balance from the start. Make time for yourself and your loved ones by engaging in activities that bring you joy and relaxation. Find a routine that works for you, whether it's a morning workout, a study session, or a nightly debrief.

Navigating Challenges

One of the biggest challenges you'll face in your first year is adapting from the guided environment of the academy and field training to navigating the unpredictable nature of real-world policing on your own. However, instead of shying away from the challenges that come your way, embrace them as an opportunity to learn and grow.

1. **Adapting to Real-World Policing:** Transition from controlled academy scenarios to unpredictable real-world situations. Stay calm under pressure and make sound decisions in real time.

2. **Dealing with Difficult Colleagues or Supervisors:** Stay focused and professional, even with challenging personalities. Learn from these experiences and maintain your composure.

3. **Handling Feedback and Criticism:** Constant feedback is meant to help you improve. Develop a thick skin, take feedback constructively, and use it as a growth tool. Handle criticism professionally.

4. **Balancing Independence and Supervision:** Find the balance between taking initiative and seeking guidance

from supervisors. Trust your training and judgment, but don't hesitate to ask for advice when needed.

Common Pitfalls to Avoid

I can't stress enough the importance of steering clear of the common pitfalls. Not only will they hinder your professional development, but they will also affect your home life. Unfortunately, I've seen too many officers lose their careers and families, and some even take their own lives due to these.

Some of the most prevalent pitfalls new officers encounter are:

1. **Alcohol Abuse:** Be mindful of the potential for alcohol abuse as a coping mechanism. Although the profession has its dangers, none amount to the damaging impact of alcohol. By no means am I saying you have to be sober, but just make sure to seek healthier ways to manage stress and emotions.
2. **Social Media:** I've seen countless officers get in trouble over social media. Be cautious about what you post because your online presence can impact your professional reputation.
3. **Affairs:** Although the devastation that can come from an affair is well-known, it continues to be a common theme in law enforcement. The turmoil of an affair combined with the stress of the job often leads to grave results.

Your first year as a law enforcement officer will shape the trajectory of your entire career. Welcome this first year as an opportunity to learn, grow, and establish yourself as the officer you aspire to be. Your dedication and hard work will lay the groundwork for a long, successful, and rewarding career.

PART V:

THE BIGGER PICTURE

Scars of Duty

I can still recall the heat on my face, the odor of gasoline soaking the asphalt, and the sound of flames crackling as I ran toward the wreckage of a vehicle. Within that chaos, the wails of children trapped inside pierced what once was a morning calmness. As I ran towards the wreckage, I slowed down momentarily, my eyes catching the gruesome sight of the driver, ejected from the vehicle and scattered across the road. I had experienced violence up close and personal throughout my life, but never had I seen anything as violent as this wreckage. My brain almost became stunned for a split second, trying to make sense of what my eyes were seeing until the screams of the children snapped my mind back into focus.

I realized the flames were growing faster than anticipated when I got to the vehicle. I sprinted back to my patrol car to get a fire extinguisher, panic setting in as I realized I had neglected to check its status—a huge complacency error on my part. Honestly, I wasn't even sure if one was inside my car. An immense amount of relief set in as the trunk popped open, and I saw that red cylinder tucked into a corner. "Please work, please work, please work," I recited as I scrambled back to the wreckage.

I tried to douse the flames while my squadmate worked on getting the children out, but it was as if the fire grew angrier at my attempts to put it out. The flames were now entirely inside the vehicle, the vehicle was still upside down, and multiple children were trapped inside. Fuck. Most officers will have at least one call that scars them for life…and I knew undoubtedly that this would be mine.

The aftermath of a devastating vehicle wreckage. The charred remains of the vehicle serve as a sobering reminder of the fragility of
life and the unpredictable dangers officers face when responding to
critical incidents. This wreckage represents not just the physical de-
struction but the emotional weight carried by those who respond
to such harrowing scenes.

Wellness

Law enforcement often focuses on physical readiness and tactical skills, but equally important is the need to maintain mental and emotional well-being. The job is demanding, exposing officers to high-stress situations, trauma, and the darker sides of human nature. Ensuring mental wellness is crucial for your professional effectiveness, personal life, and overall health.

The Importance of Mental Wellness

Staying mentally well is paramount in a profession that constantly tests your resilience and exposes you to potentially traumatic events. Law enforcement officers frequently encounter situations that most people never face in their lifetimes—responding to violent crimes, dealing with victims of abuse, witnessing fatalities, and making split-second decisions that can mean life or death. These experiences can accumulate and take a significant toll on your mental health if not properly managed.

The pressures of the job can lead to stress, anxiety, depression, and even PTSD. The constant state of alertness, the need to make quick and critical decisions, and the exposure to human suffering and violence can overwhelm even the most resilient individuals. It's not uncommon for officers to experience feelings of isolation, frustration, or hopelessness as they grapple with the demands of their role.

It's essential to recognize that these challenges are part of the reality of law enforcement, and addressing them head-on is a sign of strength, not weakness. Acknowledging your mental and emotional struggles is the first step toward healing and maintaining your overall well-being. It's important to dispel the myth that seeking help is a sign of weakness; it demonstrates self-awareness and a commitment to personal and professional growth.

Maintaining mental wellness is crucial for your personal health and your effectiveness as an officer. When your mental health is compromised, it can affect your judgment, reaction time, and ability to communicate effectively. This can put you, your colleagues, and the community you serve at risk. Prioritizing mental wellness ensures that you are functioning at your best, making sound decisions, and providing the highest level of service.

Moreover, by caring for your mental health, you set a positive example for your peers and help foster a culture of support within your department. When officers see their colleagues prioritizing mental wellness and seeking help when needed, it encourages them to do the same. This collective approach to mental health can lead to a more supportive and resilient force better equipped to handle the challenges of law enforcement.

In addition, addressing mental health issues proactively can prevent more severe consequences down the line. Untreated mental health conditions can lead to substance abuse, relationship problems, and even suicidal thoughts. By seeking help early and implementing coping strategies, you can mitigate these risks and maintain a healthier, more balanced life.

Ultimately, staying mentally well allows you to be a better officer, partner, parent, and friend. It enhances your ability to connect with others, understand their needs, and provide compassionate and effective service. In a profession where the stakes are high and the demands are relentless, investing in your mental health is one of the most important things you can do for yourself and those around you.

Seeking Help Shows Real Strength

Contrary to outdated beliefs, seeking help for mental health issues is a sign of strength and wisdom. In the past, there has been a pervasive stigma surrounding mental health in the law enforcement community, where seeking help was often viewed as a weakness or a sign of inadequacy. However, this perspective is not only outdated but also harmful. Recognizing when you are struggling and having the courage to reach out for support demonstrates true strength and resilience.

It takes immense courage to acknowledge your vulnerabilities and confront the emotional and psychological challenges of the job. Law enforcement officers are often seen as protectors and authority figures, expected to remain stoic and unshakable in adversity. Yet, behind the badge, officers are human beings who experience the full spectrum of emotions. Admitting that you need help is a profound act of self-awareness and responsibility to yourself and those you serve and protect.

Ignoring mental health issues can lead to severe consequences, both personally and professionally. Unaddressed stress, anxiety, depression, or PTSD can escalate and manifest in various detrimental ways, such as substance abuse, impaired judgment, and strained relationships. Professionally, it can affect your performance, decision-making, and interactions with colleagues and the public. Over time, these issues can erode your effectiveness as an officer and your ability to fulfill your duties safely and compassionately.

Most law enforcement agencies now offer a range of support services designed to help officers manage the unique stresses of the job. These can include:

1. **Counseling Services:** Professional counselors can provide a safe and confidential space to explore your feelings,

cope with trauma, and develop effective strategies for managing stress.

2. **Peer Support Programs:** Peer support teams consist of fellow officers trained to offer emotional and practical support. Speaking with someone who understands the challenges of the job firsthand can be incredibly validating and helpful.

3. **Mental Health Professionals:** Psychologists and psychiatrists who specialize in working with law enforcement personnel can offer expert guidance and treatment for more severe mental health issues.

4. **Employee Assistance Programs (EAPs):** EAPs provide a variety of services, including mental health support, financial counseling, and legal advice, all aimed at helping officers navigate personal and professional challenges.

5. **Chaplains and Spiritual Advisors:** For those who find solace in spirituality, chaplains can offer support, guidance, and a compassionate ear in times of need.

Embracing these resources helps you manage your mental health and sets a positive example for your peers. When officers see their colleagues taking proactive steps to care for their mental health, it can encourage them to do the same, fostering a healthier and more supportive work environment.

Seeking help can also lead to personal growth and improved relationships. By addressing your mental health needs, you become more resilient, better equipped to handle stress, and more empathetic in your interactions with others. This growth can enhance your effectiveness as an officer and positively impact your relationships with family, friends, and the community.

My Personal Journey

I have faced my share of mental and emotional challenges in this career. There were times when the weight of the job, mixed with indulging in some of the "pitfalls" I mentioned earlier in the book, came together and made my life a living hell. Unfortunately, my loved ones were left to carry the burden for a long time before I hit bottom and realized I needed help. Reaching out to chaplains and mental health professionals has been a transformative experience for me. It has not only made me a better officer but also a better father, friend, and overall person. Seeking help allowed me to process my experiences, build resilience, and develop healthier coping mechanisms.

Maintaining mental wellness is a continuous practice that requires attention and effort. By prioritizing your mental health, you not only enhance your ability to serve your community effectively but also improve your overall quality of life. Remember, seeking help is a sign of strength and an important step towards being the best person you can be on and off duty. Utilize the resources and support available, and never underestimate the power of a healthy mind.

Leaving a Legacy

A Message to Minority Officers

As you progress through your career in law enforcement, it's essential to think about the legacy you want to leave behind. The impact of your actions, the relationships you build, and the values you uphold will define how you are remembered by your colleagues, the community, and future generations of officers. Leaving a legacy is about more than just doing your job; it's about making a lasting positive difference in the lives of those you serve and those who follow in your footsteps.

As a minority officer, you will face unique challenges. I know firsthand the obstacles you may face, the doubts that might arise, and the pressures that come with wearing the badge. But I also know the incredible impact you can have on your community and the legacy you can leave behind.

When I first entered law enforcement, I was acutely aware of the skepticism and scrutiny that came with my identity. There were moments when I felt isolated and moments when I questioned my place. You can't *not* notice when you're the only black officer in the briefing room before shift, or one of three on an entire SWAT team, or a whole list of many other instances. However, I was reminded of my strength and purpose during these times of adversity. I realized that my presence in law enforcement was not just about fulfilling a role but about breaking barriers and setting an example for others who look like me.

Your journey will not be easy. You may encounter bias, both subtle and overt. There will be times when you feel like you have to prove yourself repeatedly. But remember, you are not alone. Many have walked this path before you and thrived despite the challenges. Use our stories as a source of inspiration and a reminder that you can succeed.

One of the most powerful tools at your disposal is your ability to build bridges. Your unique perspective allows you to connect with communities that may feel marginalized or mistrustful of law enforcement. You can show them that officers can be compassionate, understanding, and dedicated to justice for all. Your interactions can change perceptions and foster a sense of trust and cooperation that benefits everyone.

Stay true to your values and maintain your integrity, even when difficult. Your commitment to doing what is right, even in the face of adversity, will set you apart and earn you the respect of your colleagues and community. Lead by example, and let your actions speak louder than any words.

Lastly, never lose sight of your "why." Your reason for joining law enforcement is your anchor. Whether it is to protect your community, to be a role model, or to bring about positive change, hold onto that purpose. It will guide you through the toughest days and remind you why your presence in this profession is so vital.

You are a trailblazer, a bridge-builder, and a beacon of hope for many. Your journey is not just about you but about paving the way for future generations of minority officers. Stand tall, stay strong, and remember the difference you make. Your contribution to law enforcement is invaluable, and your impact will be felt for years to come.

The Future of Policing

The landscape of law enforcement is ever-evolving, shaped by societal changes, technological advancements, and shifting public expectations. As we look to the future of policing, it is clear that our profession must adapt and grow to meet these new challenges while staying true to its core mission of protecting and serving the community. Adapting to this evolution is essential for building a more effective, transparent, and community-oriented police force.

The future of policing lies in strengthening the relationship between law enforcement and the communities we serve. Community policing is not a new concept, but it is becoming increasingly important as we strive to build trust and collaboration. Engaging with community members, understanding their concerns, and working together to find solutions are crucial to modern policing. By being present and accessible in the community, officers can build relationships beyond enforcement, creating a sense of partnership and shared responsibility for public safety.

I know firsthand how easy it is to overlook this aspect of policing. The last thing on my mind when I was working in an extremely violent and busy neighborhood was to take a minute to talk with someone just for the hell of it. It took years before I recognized the importance of doing just that. You might get a few "F pigs" responses depending on who you contact. Still, if you change just one person's perception of police officers out of every twenty you contact, I'd say it's worth it. Too often, an individual's only experience with an officer is during enforcement, investigations, or what they see in the media. You can change this. Never forget that.

Thank You

As we conclude this roadmap together, I want to extend my heartfelt gratitude to you, the reader. Thank you for taking the time to read this book.

Your decision to pursue this noble profession speaks volumes about your character, dedication, and willingness to serve your community. By choosing this career, you are stepping into a role that has the power to make a significant and positive impact on countless lives.

I hope the insights, stories, and guidance shared within these pages have given you valuable knowledge and inspiration. Remember to always keep your "why" at the forefront of your mind, strive for excellence, and approach each day with a mindset of growth and service.

You are stepping into a career that will be filled with challenges but also with incredible rewards. Stay true to your values, maintain your integrity, and never underestimate the importance of your role in shaping the future of law enforcement.

Thank you for your dedication to this profession and commitment to making a difference. May your career be fulfilling, impactful, and guided by the principles shared within this book.

Stay safe, stay strong, and always remember the legacy you are building.

My SWAT teammate and I scout the scene during a mission involving an armed barricaded suspect. This moment captures the intensity and teamwork required to ensure mission success.

Acknowledgments

To my mother, the visionary of my life's achievements. Thank you for being my unwavering supporter, the cornerstone of my success.

To my brother, without whom, my life would have certainly taken a very different path. Thank you for pushing, guiding, and always being there when I needed you most.

To my Aunt, thank you for always answering my calls. Our talks have been a lifeline.

Uncle M, your early influence has been a guiding light, shaping the person I have become.

"Ryan Parker," few are willing to take a rookie under their arms and show them the ropes as you did. Thank you. That first shift together was nothing short of cinematic.

To my other car partners on patrol, S.M., J.K., and A.F., your support and vigilance kept me safe and, more importantly, sane throughout countless shifts. "Thank you" doesn't do justice.

A special thanks to my lifelong friend Jordan for narrating the videos for this book. May you continue to grow and thrive in your own way, just as you have helped me grow in mine.

While I wish to name everyone who has impacted my career, that would fill another chapter entirely. To Uncle V, my P8 family, and many others, know that your influences resonate deeply within me.

Lastly, I know this might be a bit unorthodox, but I want to thank myself. The people closest to me know the trials and tribulations I faced writing this book. Some by my own doing...like deciding to write this while also being a full-time college student and full-time police officer. Others were completely out of my hands.

Then there were the doubts. Whether from the fear of wondering what others may say or my own questions about whether I was qualified to write something like this. Whatever it was, I always seemed to face a new hurdle whenever I felt the end of the book nearing. That's when I knew I was on to something good and had to keep pushing. Thankfully, with encouragement from my loved ones, I was able to complete it.

You might have read this and have no desire to write a book but have another passion you wish to pursue. It might be a hobby you want to turn into a business or a position you want to apply for. Whatever it is, don't let anything or anyone hold you back from pursuing it. The outcome doesn't matter as much as the fact that you actually did it. If no one else has encouraged you, let me be the first...go crush it.

About the Author

E.J. Cooper has dedicated his entire adult life to service. His journey began in the ranks of the United States Marine Corps, where the discipline and leadership forged became the foundation on which he built his career. His path of honorable service continued into the Air Force Reserve while simultaneously embarking on a career in law enforcement.

Cooper's experience spans several law enforcement agencies across various states, from the bustling streets of metropolitan cities to the quiet suburbs. He has served in multiple capacities, including Patrol Officer, Field Training Officer, Defensive Tactics Instructor, SWAT (Special Weapons and Tactics), and Patrol Sergeant. His mission doesn't stop at uniformed service; it extends into sharing the lessons he's learned through writing with the debut of his first book, *The Rookie Handbook: How to Become the Officer Every Department Wants and Every Community Needs.*